Learn the Essentials of The Elliott Wave Principle in 30 Minutes

by Robert R. Prechter

Elliott Wave International

www.elliottwave.com

Learn the Essentials of The Elliott Wave Principle in 30 Minutes
Copyright © 1978-2024 Robert R. Prechter

Printed in the United States of America

ISBN: 978-1-61604-141-0

Publisher: New Classics Library
www.elliottwave.com

CONTENTS

FOREWORD

The Wave Principle allows an analyst to anticipate large and small shifts in the psychology driving any investment market and helps minimize the emotions that drive investment decisions. Where did this valuable tool come from?

Ralph Nelson Elliott, a corporate accountant by profession, discovered that financial markets adhere to a fractal price structure. Using his discovery, he made astonishingly accurate stock market forecasts between 1934 and 1946. He called his discovery "the Wave Principle."

Robert Prechter resurrected the Wave Principle from near obscurity in 1976. He was working as an analyst for Merrill Lynch when he located microfilm copies of R.N. Elliott's books in the New York Public Library. Prechter and A.J. Frost collaborated on *Elliott Wave Principle* in 1978. The book became a Wall Street bestseller and has been translated into a dozen languages. The current pamphlet derives from that book. For those interested in further exploration of the Wave Principle, resources are available at the following addresses:

> www.elliottwave.com/books
> www.elliottwave.com/videos
> www.elliottwave.com
> www.socionomics.net
> www.robertprechter.com

THE BASICS

"The Wave Principle" is Ralph Nelson Elliott's discovery that social, or crowd, behavior trends and reverses in recognizable patterns. Using stock market data for the Dow Jones Industrial Average (DJIA) as his main research tool, Elliott discovered that the ever-changing path of stock mar-ket prices reveals a structural design that in turn reflects fractal structures found in nature.

Elliott isolated thirteen patterns of directional movement, called *waves*, that recur in markets and are repetitive in form but not necessarily in time or amplitude. He named, defined and illustrated the patterns. He then described how these structures link together to form larger versions of the same patterns, how those in turn are the building blocks for patterns of the next larger size, and so on. His descriptions led to a set of empirically derived rules and guidelines for interpreting market action. The patterns that naturally occur under the Wave Principle are described below.

THE FIVE-WAVE PATTERN

In markets, progress ultimately takes the form of five waves of a specific structure. Three of these waves, which are labeled 1, 3 and 5, actually effect the directional movement. They are separated by two countertrend interruptions, which are labeled 2 and 4, as shown in Figure 1. The two interruptions are apparently a requisite for overall directional movement to occur.

At any time, the market may be identified as being somewhere in the basic five-wave pattern at the largest degree of trend. Because the five-wave pattern is the overriding form of market progress, all other patterns are subsumed by it.

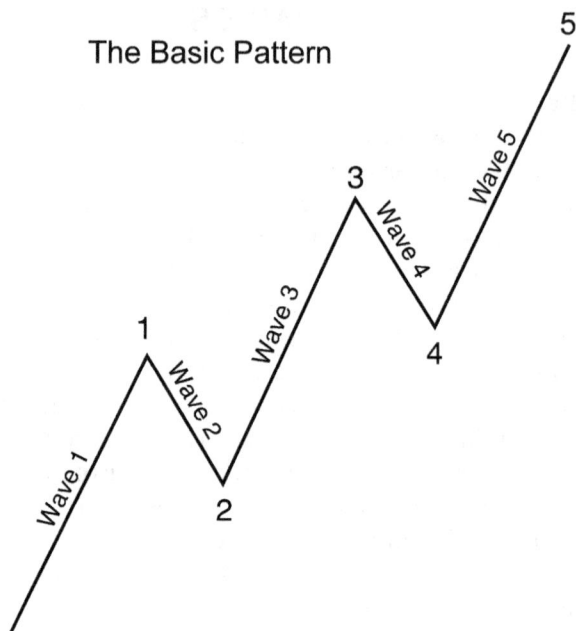

The Basic Pattern

Figure 1

WAVE MODE

There are two modes of wave development: *motive* and *corrective*. Motive waves have a *five*-wave structure, while corrective waves have a *three*-wave structure or a variation thereof. Motive mode is employed by both the five-wave pattern of Figure 1 *and* its same-directional components, i.e., waves 1, 3 and 5. Corrective mode is employed by all countertrend interruptions, which include waves 2 and 4 in Figure 1. "Corrective" waves accomplish only a partial retracement of the progress achieved by any preceding motive wave. The two modes are fundamentally different, both in their roles and in their construction.

The five-wave motive phase has subwaves denoted by numbers, and the three-wave corrective phase has subwaves are denoted by letters. Every motive wave is

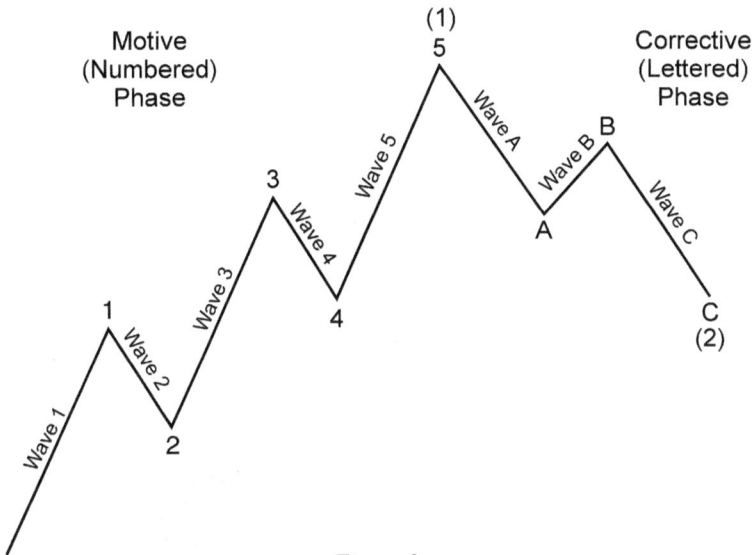

Figure 2

followed by a corrective wave. Just as wave 2 corrects wave 1 in Figure 1, the sequence A, B, C corrects the sequence 1, 2, 3, 4, 5 in Figure 2.

THE ESSENTIAL DESIGN

Figure 3 not only illustrates a *larger* version of Figure 2, it also illustrates *Figure 2 itself*, in greater detail. Waves (1) and (2) in Figure 3, if examined under a "microscope," would take the same form as waves ① and ②. Regardless of degree, the form is constant. We can use Figure 3 to illustrate two waves, eight waves or thirty-four waves, depending upon the degree to which we are referring.

Within the corrective pattern illustrated as wave ② in Figure 3, waves (A) and (C), which point downward, each comprise five waves: 1, 2, 3, 4 and 5. Similarly, wave (B), which points upward, comprises three waves: A, B and C. This construction discloses a crucial point: Motive waves

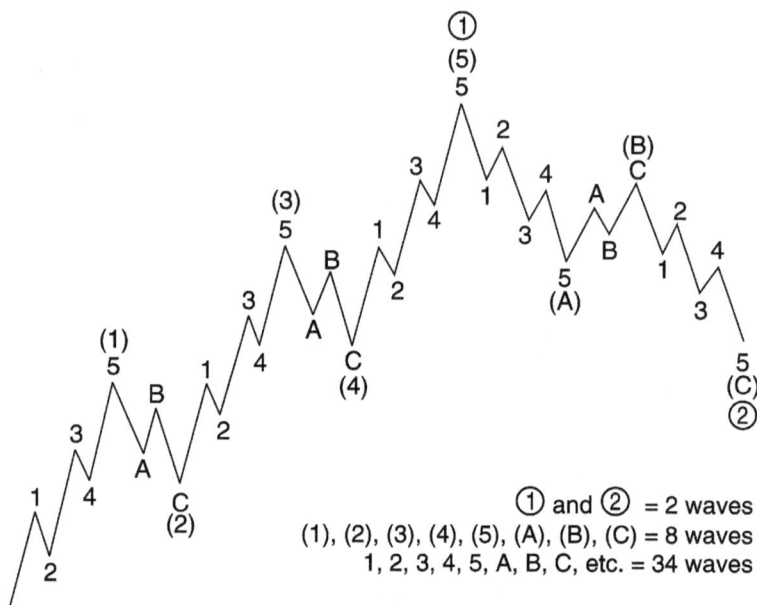

Figure 3

do not always point upward, and corrective waves do not always point downward. The mode of a wave is determined not by its absolute direction but by its *relative* direction. Aside from four specific exceptions, which will be discussed later in this chapter, waves divide in *motive* mode (five waves) when trending in the same direction as the wave of one larger degree of which it is a part, and in *corrective* mode (three waves or a variation) when trending in the opposite direction. Waves (A) and (C) are motive, trending in the *same direction* as wave ②. Wave (B) is corrective because it is *countertrend* to wave ②. In summary, the essential underlying tendency of the Wave Principle is that *action in the same direction as the one larger trend develops in five waves, while reaction against the one larger trend develops in three waves,* at all degrees of trend.

Nor does Figure 3 imply finality. As before, this larger cycle automatically becomes two subdivisions of the wave of *next* higher degree. As long as progress continues, the process of building to greater degrees continues. The reverse process of subdividing into lesser degrees apparently continues indefinitely as well. As far as we can determine, then, all waves both *have* and *are* component waves.

VARIATIONS ON THE BASIC THEME

The Wave Principle would be simple to apply if the basic theme described above were the complete description of market behavior. However, the real world, fortunately or unfortunately, is not so simple. The rest of this section fills out the details of how the market behaves.

WAVE DEGREE

All waves may be categorized by relative size, or degree. Elliott discerned nine degrees of waves, from the smallest wiggle on an hourly chart to the largest wave he could assume existed from the data then available. He chose the names listed below to label these degrees, from largest to smallest:

Grand Supercycle
Supercycle
Cycle
Primary
Intermediate
Minor
Minute
Minuette
Subminuette

Cycle waves subdivide into Primary waves that subdivide into Intermediate waves that in turn subdivide into Minor and sub-Minor waves. It is important to understand that these labels refer to specifically identifiable degrees of waves. By using this nomenclature, the analyst can identify precisely the position of a wave in the overall progression of the market, much as longitude and latitude are used to identify a geographical location. To say, "the Dow Jones Industrial Average is in Minute wave ⓥ of Minor wave 1 of Intermediate wave (3) of Primary wave ⑤ of Cycle wave I of Supercycle wave (V) of the current Grand Supercycle" is to identify a specific point along the progression of market history.

When numbering and lettering waves, some scheme such as the one shown below is recommended to differentiate the degrees of waves in the stock market's progression. We have standardized the labels as follows:

Wave Degree	5s With the Trend					3s Against the Trend		
Grand Supercycle	Ⓘ	Ⓘ	Ⓘ	Ⓘ	Ⓥ	ⓐ	ⓑ	ⓒ
Supercycle	(I)	(II)	(III)	(IV)	(V)	(a)	(b)	(c)
Cycle	I	II	III	IV	V	a	b	c
Primary	①	②	③	④	⑤	Ⓐ	Ⓑ	Ⓒ
Intermediate	(1)	(2)	(3)	(4)	(5)	(A)	(B)	(C)
Minor	1	2	3	4	5	A	B	C
Minute	ⓘ	ⓘ	ⓘ	ⓘ	ⓥ	ⓐ	ⓑ	ⓒ
Minuette	(i)	(ii)	(iii)	(iv)	(v)	(a)	(b)	(c)
Subminuette	i	ii	iii	iv	v	a	b	c

MOTIVE WAVES

Motive waves subdivide into *five* waves and always move in the same direction as the trend of one larger degree. They are straightforward and relatively easy to recognize and interpret.

Within motive waves, wave 2 always retraces less than 100% of wave 1, and wave 4 always retraces less than 100% of wave 3. Wave 3, moreover, always travels beyond the end of wave 1. The goal of a motive wave is to make progress, and these rules of formation assure that it will.

Elliott discovered that in price terms, wave 3 is often the longest and never the shortest among the three actionary waves (1, 3 and 5) of a motive wave. As long as wave 3 undergoes a greater percentage movement than either wave 1 or 5, this rule is satisfied. It almost always holds on an arithmetic basis as well. There are two types of motive waves: *impulse* and *diagonal*.

IMPULSE

The most common motive wave is an *impulse*. In an impulse, wave 4 does not enter the territory of (i.e., "overlap") wave 1. This rule holds for all non-leveraged "cash" markets. Futures markets, with their extreme leverage, can induce short term price extremes that would not occur in cash markets. Even so, overlap is usually confined to daily and intraday price fluctuations and even then is rare. In addition, the actionary subwaves (1, 3 and 5) of an impulse are themselves motive, and subwave 3 is specifically an impulse. Figures 2, 3 and 4 depict impulses in the 1, 3, 5, A and C wave positions.

As detailed in the preceding three paragraphs, there are only a few simple rules for interpreting impulses properly. A *rule* is so called because it governs all waves to which it applies. Typical, *yet not inevitable*, characteristics of waves are called *guidelines*. Guidelines of impulse formation, including extension, truncation, alternation,

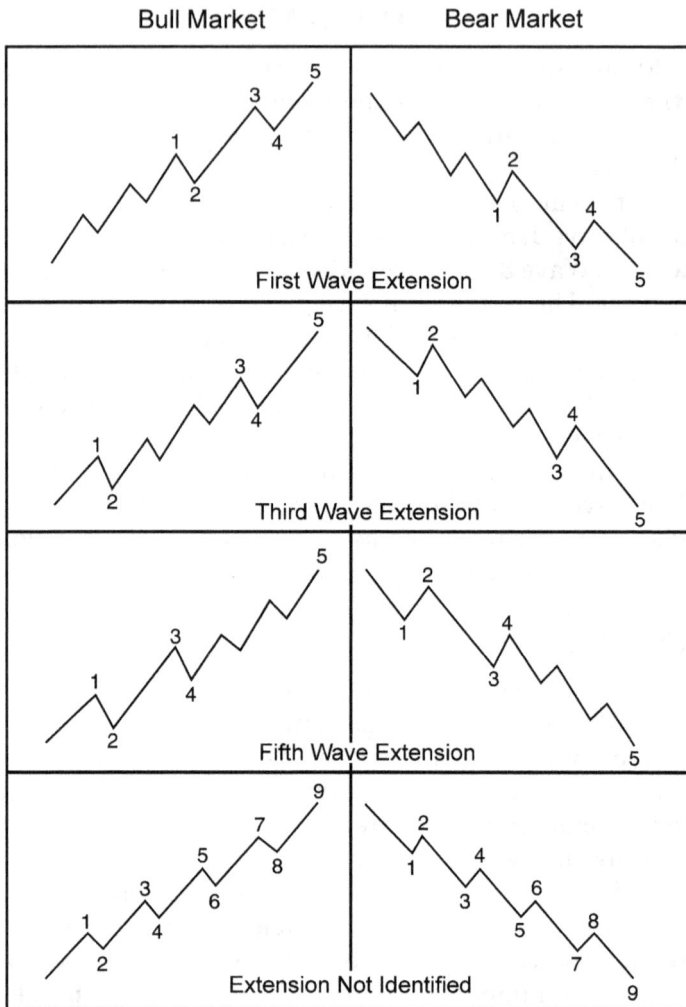

Figure 4

equality, channeling, personality and ratio relationships are discussed below. Rules and guidelines have great practical utility in correct counting, which we will explore further in discussing extensions.

Extension

Most impulses contain what Elliott called an extension. Extensions are elongated impulses with exaggerated subdivisions. The vast majority of impulse waves do contain an extension in one and only one of their three motive subwaves (1, 3 or 5). The diagrams in Figure 4, illustrating extensions, will clarify this point.

Often the third wave of an extended third wave is an extension, producing a profile such as shown in Figure 5.

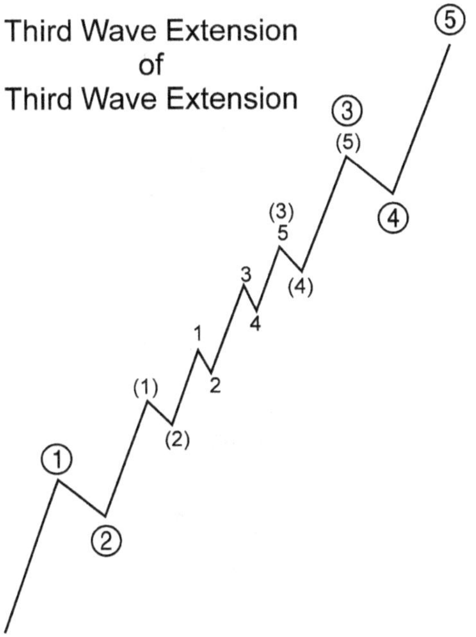

Figure 5

Truncation

"Truncation" describes a situation in which the fifth wave does not move beyond the end of the third. A truncation can usually be verified by noting that the presumed fifth wave contains the necessary five subwaves, as illustrated in Figures 6 and 7. Truncation often occurs following a particularly strong third wave.

Truncation gives warning of underlying weakness or strength in the market. In application, a truncated fifth wave will often cut short an expected target. This annoyance is counterbalanced by its clear implications for persistence in the new direction of trend.

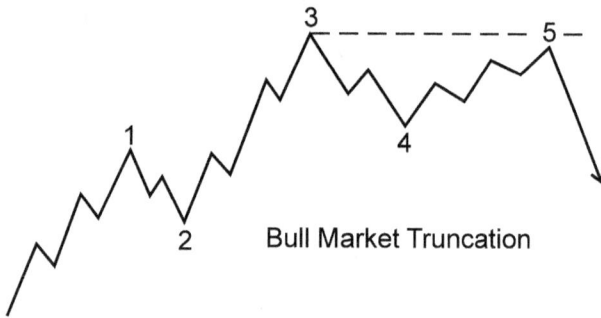

Bull Market Truncation

Figure 6

Bear Market Truncation

Figure 7

DIAGONALS

A diagonal is a motive pattern, yet not an impulse, as it has corrective characteristics, namely, three-wave subdivisions and overlap. Diagonals substitute for impulses at specific locations in the wave structure. An ending diagonal (see Figure 8) is a special type of wave that occurs in the fifth wave position at times when the preceding move has gone "too far too fast," as Elliott put it.

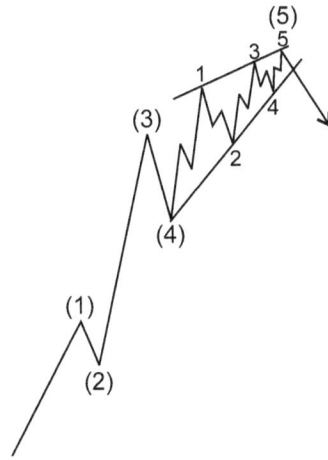

Prechter observed that a diagonal occasionally appears in the wave 1 position of impulses and in the wave A position of zigzags. In the few examples we have, the subdivisions of a leading diagonal appear to be 3-3-3-3-3, although in some cases, they can be labeled 5-3-5-3-5, so the jury is out on a strict definition. Analysts must be aware of this pattern to avoid mistaking it for a far more common development, a series of first and second waves. A leading diagonal in the wave one position is typically followed by a deep retracement.

Figure 8

CORRECTIVE WAVES

Markets move *against* the trend of one greater degree only with a seeming struggle. Resistance from the larger trend appears to prevent a correction from developing a motive structure. The struggle between the two oppositely trending degrees generally makes corrective waves less clearly identifiable than motive waves, which always flow with comparative ease in the direction of the one larger trend. As another result of the conflict between trends, corrective waves are quite a bit more varied than motive waves. Corrective patterns fall into four main categories:

> *Zigzag* (5-3-5; includes two types: single and double);
> *Flat* (3-3-5; three types: regular, expanded, and running);
> *Triangle (3-3-3-3-3;* three types: contracting, barrier and expanding; and a variation of contracting: running);
> *Combination* (called a double three).

ZIGZAGS (5-3-5)

A *single zigzag* in a bull market is a simple three-wave declining pattern labeled A-B-C and subdividing 5-3-5. The top of wave B is noticeably lower than the start of wave A, as illustrated in Figures 9 and 10.

Occasionally zigzags will occur twice in succession, particularly when the first zigzag falls short of a normal target. In these cases, each zigzag is separated by an intervening "three" (labeled X), producing what is called a *double zigzag* (see Figure 11). The zigzags are labeled W and Y.

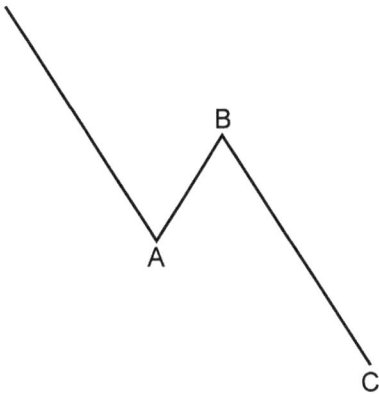

Figure 9

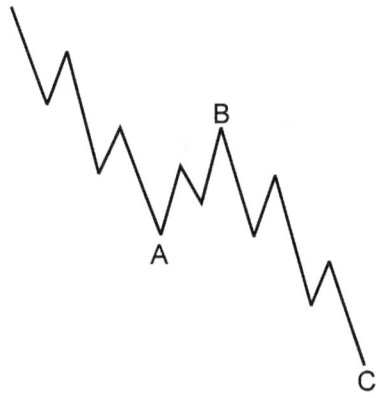

Figure 10

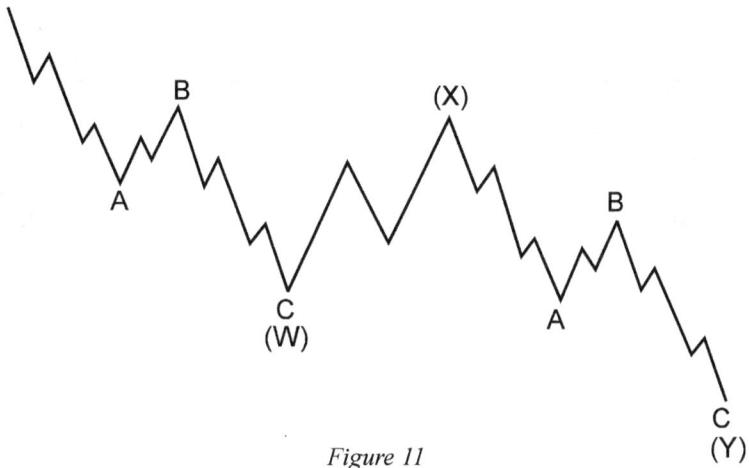

Figure 11

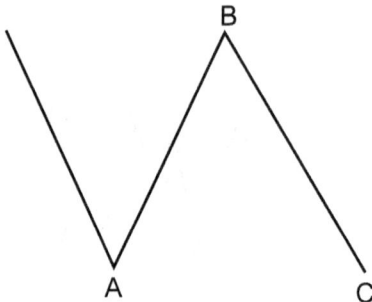

Figure 12

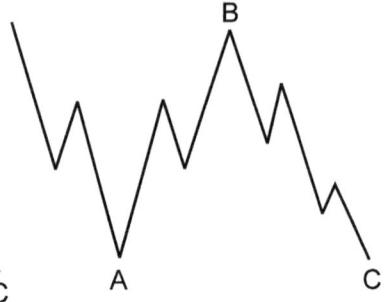

Figure 13

FLATS (3-3-5)

A flat correction differs from a zigzag in that the subwave sequence is 3-3-5, as shown in Figures 13 and 15. Since wave A lacks sufficient downward force to unfold into a full five waves as it does in a zigzag, the B wave reaction seems to inherit this lack of countertrend pressure and terminates near the start of wave A. Wave C, in turn, generally terminates just slightly beyond the end of wave A rather than significantly beyond as in zigzags.

Flat corrections usually retrace less of preceding impulse waves than do zigzags. They participate in periods

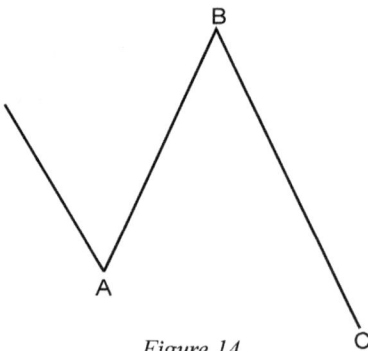

Figure 14

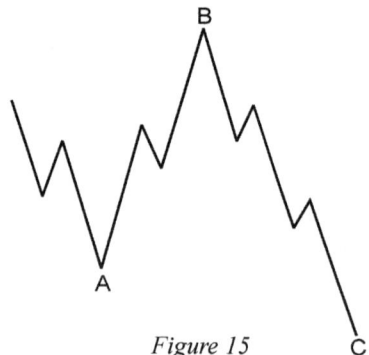

Figure 15

involving a strong larger trend and thus virtually always precede or follow extensions. The more powerful the underlying trend, the briefer the flat tends to be. Within impulses, fourth waves frequently sport flats, while second waves rarely do.

Three types of 3-3-5 corrections have been identified by differences in their overall shape. In a *regular* flat correction, wave B terminates about at the level of the beginning of wave A, and wave C terminates a slight bit past the end of wave A, as we have shown in Figures 12 and 13. Far more common, however, is the variety called an *expanded* flat, which contains a price extreme beyond that of the preceding impulse wave. In expanded flats, wave B of the 3-3-5 pattern terminates beyond the starting level of wave A, and wave C ends more substantially beyond the ending level of wave A, as shown in Figures 14 and 15.

In a rare variation on the 3-3-5 pattern, which we call a *running* flat, wave B terminates well beyond the beginning of wave A as in an expanded flat, but wave C fails to travel its full distance, falling short of the level at which wave A ended.

TRIANGLES

A triangle appears to reflect a balance of forces, causing a sideways movement. The triangle pattern contains five overlapping waves that subdivide 3-3-3-3-3 and are labeled A-B-C-D-E. Triangles fall into three main categories as illustrated in Figure 16. These illustrations depict the contracting and barrier triangles as taking place within the area of preceding price action, in what may be termed *regular* triangles. However, it is quite common for wave B of a contracting triangle to exceed the start of wave A in what may be termed a *running* triangle, as shown in Figure 17. In running triangles, wave E still ends within the territory of the preceding impulse.

Variations of Elliott Wave Triangles

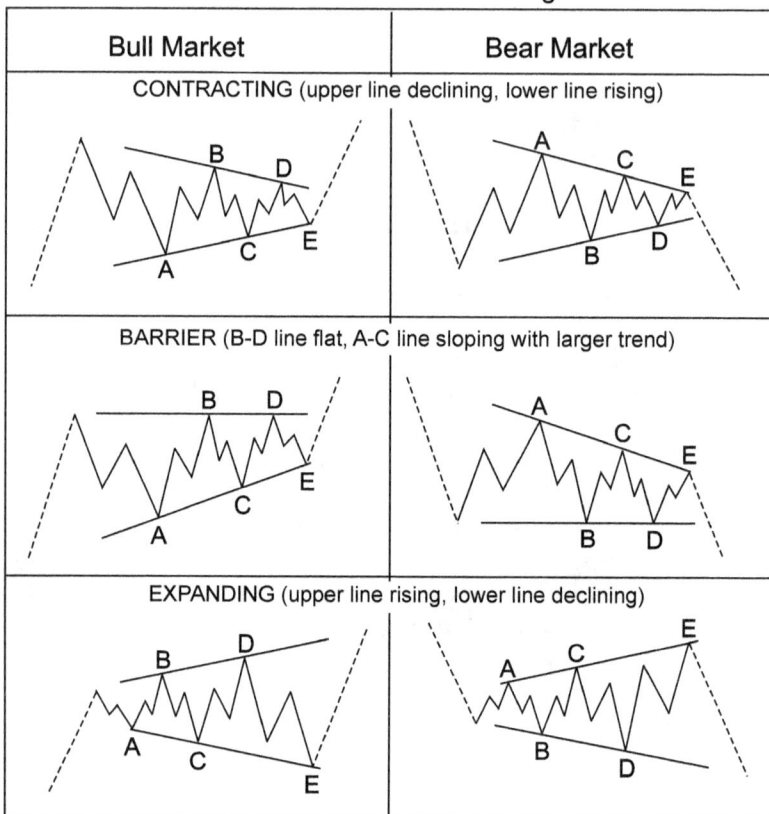

Figure 16

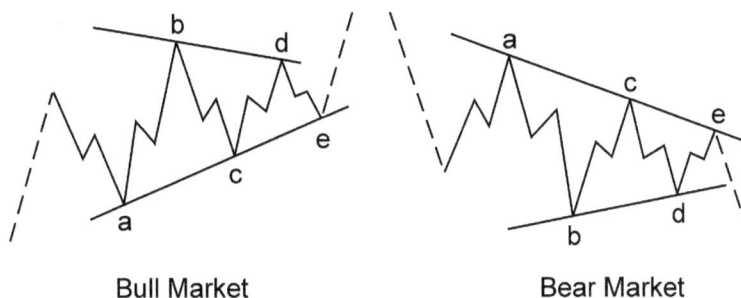

Bull Market   Bear Market

Figure 17

A triangle usually occurs in a position prior to the final actionary wave in the pattern of one larger degree, i.e., as wave four in an impulse, wave B in an A-B-C, or wave X in a double zigzag. But it can also occur as wave Y in a combination (see next section).

COMBINATIONS (DOUBLE THREES)

A double three is a combination of simpler types of corrections, including the various types of zigzags, flats and triangles. Their occurrence appears to be the flat correction's way of extending sideways action. As with double zigzags, the simple corrective patterns are labeled W and Y. The reactionary wave, labeled X, can take the shape of any corrective pattern but is most commonly a zigzag. Figures 18 and 19 show two examples of double threes.

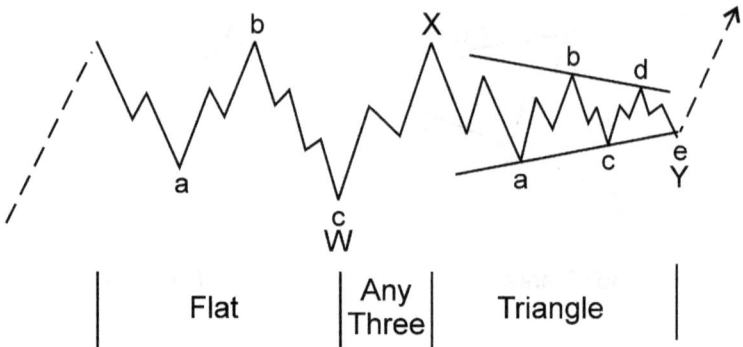

| | Flat | | Any Three | | Triangle | |

Figure 18

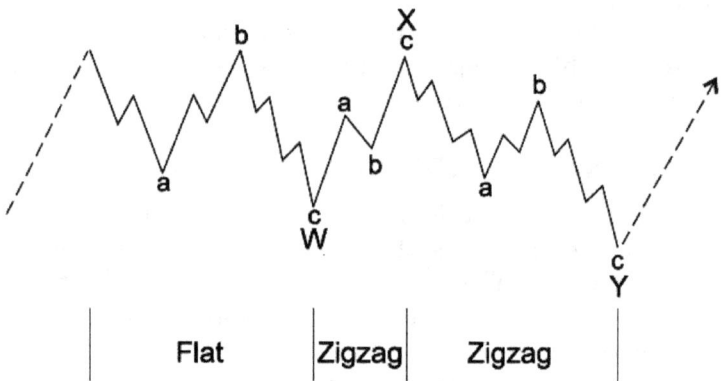

| | Flat | | Zigzag | | Zigzag | |

Figure 19

For the most part, double threes are horizontal in character. One reason for this trait is that there is never more than one zigzag in a combination. Neither is there more than one triangle. Triangles appear only as wave Y in a double three.

All the patterns illustrated in this booklet take the same form whether within a larger rising or falling trend. In a falling trend, they are simply inverted.

GUIDELINES OF WAVE FORMATION

ALTERNATION

The guideline of alternation states that if wave two of an impulse is a sharp retracement, expect wave four to be a sideways correction, and vice versa. Figure 20 shows the most characteristic breakdowns of impulse waves, both up and down. Sharp corrections never include a new price extreme, i.e., one that lies beyond the orthodox end of the preceding impulse wave. They are almost always zigzags (single or double). Sideways corrections include flats, triangles and double threes. They usually include a new price extreme, i.e., one that lies beyond the orthodox end of the preceding impulse wave.

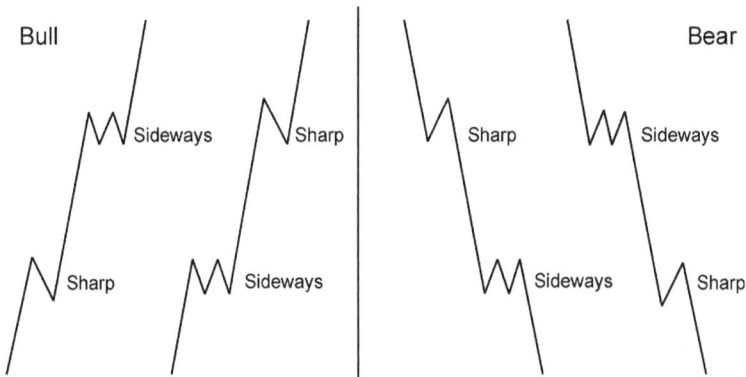

Bull   Bear

Sideways   Sharp   Sharp   Sideways

Sharp   Sideways   Sideways   Sharp

Figure 20

DEPTH OF CORRECTIVE WAVES

No market approach other than the Wave Principle gives as satisfactory an answer to the question, "How far down can a bear market be expected to go?" The primary guideline is that corrections, especially when themselves are fourth waves, tend to register their maximum retracement within the span of travel of the previous fourth wave of one lesser degree, most commonly near the level of its terminus. Note in Figure 21, for instance, how wave 2 ends at the level of wave four of 1, and how wave 4 ends at the level of wave four of 3.

CHANNELING TECHNIQUE

Elliott noted that parallel trend channels often mark the upper and lower boundaries of impulse waves. To draw a proper channel, connect the ends of waves two and four. Draw a parallel line starting at the end of wave 3, as shown in Figure 21.

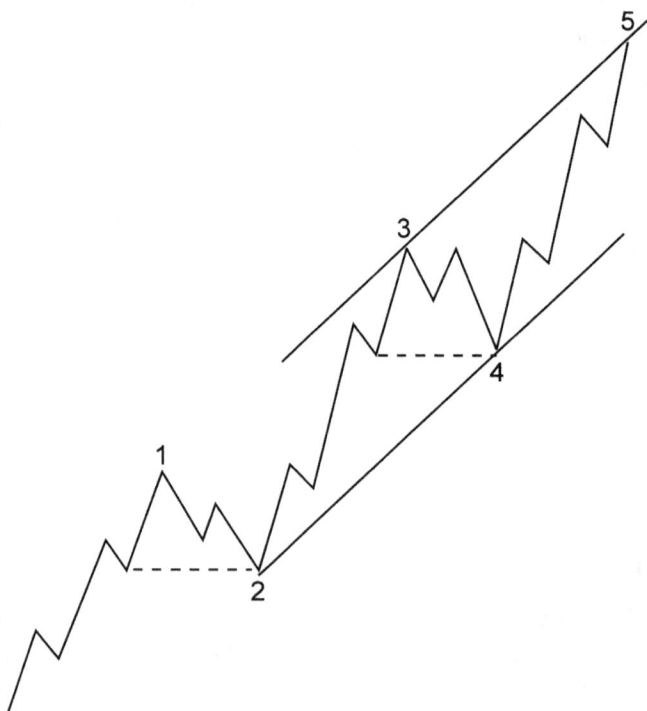

Figure 21

The question of whether to expect a parallel channel on arithmetic or semilog (percentage) scale is still unresolved as far as developing a definite tenet on the subject. If the price development at any point does not fall neatly within two parallel lines on the scale you are using, switch to the other scale in order to observe the channel in correct perspective. To stay on top of all developments, the analyst should always use both. Figures 22 and 23 show real-life channels for each type of scale.

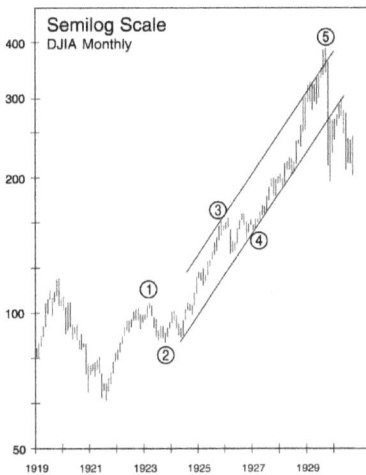 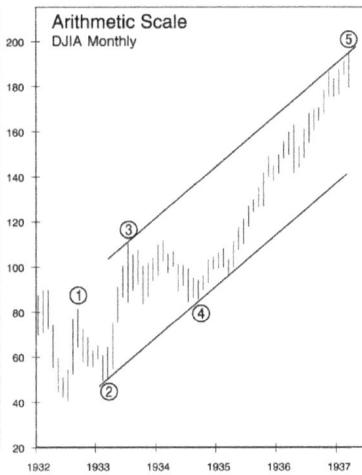

Figure 22   *Figure 23*

Within parallel channels and the converging lines of diagonal triangles, if a fifth wave approaches its upper trendline on declining volume, it is an indication that the end of the wave will meet or fall short of it. If volume is heavy as the fifth wave approaches its upper trendline, it indicates a possible penetration of the upper line, which Elliott called "throw-over." Throw-overs also occur, with the same characteristics, in declining markets.

PSYCHOLOGY OF WAVES

Elliott waves reflect mass psychological states. Figures 24 and 25 summarize some of their characteristics. (For detailed discussions of each type of wave, see Chapter 2 of *Elliott Wave Principle*.)

Idealized Elliott Wave Progression

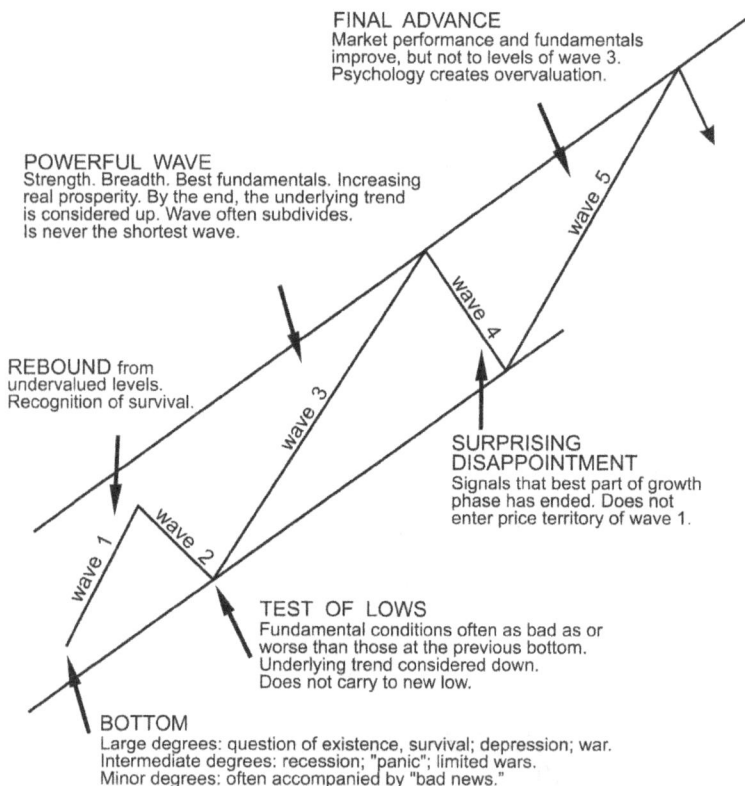

FINAL ADVANCE
Market performance and fundamentals improve, but not to levels of wave 3. Psychology creates overvaluation.

POWERFUL WAVE
Strength. Breadth. Best fundamentals. Increasing real prosperity. By the end, the underlying trend is considered up. Wave often subdivides. Is never the shortest wave.

REBOUND from undervalued levels. Recognition of survival.

SURPRISING DISAPPOINTMENT
Signals that best part of growth phase has ended. Does not enter price territory of wave 1.

TEST OF LOWS
Fundamental conditions often as bad as or worse than those at the previous bottom. Underlying trend considered down. Does not carry to new low.

BOTTOM
Large degrees: question of existence, survival; depression; war. Intermediate degrees: recession; "panic"; limited wars. Minor degrees: often accompanied by "bad news."

Figure 24

Idealized Corrective Wave

TOP
Large degrees: prosperity and peace appear
guaranteed forever. Arrogant complacency reigns.
Intermediate degrees: economic
improvement, good feeling.
Minor degrees: often accompanied by
"good news."

NARROW, EMOTIONAL ADVANCE
Technically weak, selective.
Results in non-confirmations.
Fundamentals weaken subtly.
Aggressive euphoria and denial.

TECHNICAL BREAKDOWN
Trendlines broken.
Viewed as buying opportunity.

Wave A

Wave B

Wave C

WORST OF BEAR MARKET
Strength. Breadth.
Prices decline relentlessly.
Fundamentals ultimately
collapse in response.

Figure 25

LEARNING THE BASICS

The Wave Principle is unparalleled in providing an overall perspective on the position of the market most of the time. While this perspective is extremely comforting and useful, the more practical goal of any analytical method is to identify market lows suitable for entering positions on the long side and market highs offering the opportunity to take profits or enter the short side. The Wave Principle is well suited to these functions. Nevertheless, the Wave Principle does not provide *certainty* about any market outcome.

What the Wave Principle provides is an objective means of assessing the relative *probabilities* of possible future paths for the market. Competent analysts applying the rules and guidelines of the Wave Principle objectively should usually agree on the *order* of those probabilities. At any time, two or more valid wave interpretations are usually acceptable by the *rules* of the Wave Principle. The rules are highly specific and keep the number of valid alternatives to a minimum. Among the valid alternatives, the analyst will generally regard as preferred the interpretation that satisfies the largest number of *guidelines* and will accord top alternate status to the interpretation satisfying the next largest number of guidelines, and so on.

Alternate interpretations are important. Your second-best "count" is an aspect of trading with the Wave Principle, because in the event that the market fails to follow the preferred scenario, your top alternate count becomes your backup plan.

The best approach is deductive reasoning. By applying all the characteristics of extensions, alternation, overlapping, channeling, volume and the rest, the analyst has a much more formidable arsenal than one might imagine at first glance.

Most other approaches to market analysis, whether fundamental, technical or cyclical, disallow other than arbitrarily chosen loss-limiting stop points, thus keeping either risk or frequency of stop-outs high. The Wave Principle, in contrast, provides a built-in objective method for placing a stop. Since Elliott wave analysis is based upon price patterns, a pattern identified as having been completed is either over or it isn't. If the market changes direction, the analyst has caught the turn. If the market moves beyond what the apparently completed pattern allows, the conclusion is wrong, requiring immediate adjustment.

When there is no clearly preferred interpretation, the analyst must wait until the count resolves. Subsequent waves will eventually clarify the status of previous ones.

The ability to identify junctures is remarkable enough, but the Wave Principle is the only method of analysis which also provides guidelines for forecasting. If indeed markets are patterned, and if those patterns have a recognizable quasi-geometry, then regardless of the variations allowed, certain price and time relationships are likely to recur. In fact, real world experience shows that they do. The next section addresses some additional guidelines that are helpful in the forecasting exercise.

THE FIBONACCI SEQUENCE AND ITS APPLICATION

Known for centuries by scientists, naturalists and mathematicians, the sequence of numbers 1, 1, 2, 3, 5, 8, 13, 21, 34, 55, 89, 144, and so on to infinity is known today as the Fibonacci sequence. The sum of any two adjacent numbers in this sequence forms the next higher number in the sequence, viz., 1 plus 1 equals 2, 1 plus 2 equals 3, 2 plus 3 equals 5, 3 plus 5 equals 8, and so on. The ratio of any two consecutive numbers in the sequence approximates 1.618, or its inverse, .618, after the first several numbers.

1.618 (or .618) is known as the Golden Ratio or Golden Mean. Nature uses the Golden Ratio in its most intimate building blocks and in its most advanced patterns. It is involved in such diverse phenomena as quasicrystal arrangements, planetary distances and periods, reflections of light beams on glass, the brain and nervous system, and the structures of plants and animals. The stock market has the same mathematical base as do these natural phenomena.

At every degree of stock market activity, a bull market subdivides into five waves and a bear market subdivides into three waves, giving us the 5-3 relationship that is the mathematical basis of the Wave Principle. If we start with the simplest expression of the concept of a bear swing, we get one straight-line decline. A bull swing, in its simplest form, is one straight-line advance. A complete cycle is two lines. In the next degree of complexity, the corresponding numbers are 3, 5 and 8. As illustrated in Figure 26, this sequence can be taken to infinity.

In its broadest sense, then, the Wave Principle proposes that the same law that shapes life forms is inherent in the human social experience. The Wave Principle shows up in the stock market because it is a nearly perfect recording of humanity's social-psychological states and trends, which determine patterns of progress and regress.

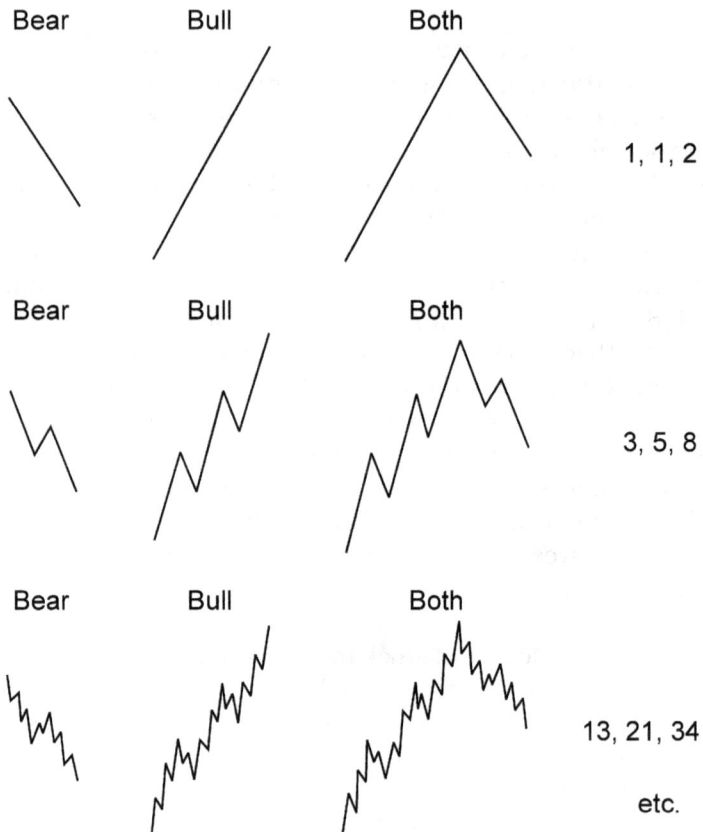

Figure 26

RATIO ANALYSIS

Because of that property, the price lengths of Elliott waves are often related to each other by a Fibonacci multiple. Adjacent waves are where most analysts and computer programs focus, but they rarely achieve perfect ratios.

Far more reliable are relationships between *alternate* waves. When wave 5 is extended, its price length can approximate 1.618 times the net distance of waves 1 through 3. Within zigzags, waves A and C are often related by equality or 1.618. Within expanded flats, wave C tends to be 1.618 times wave A. Within triangles, two alternate waves (usually either A and C, or B and D) are typically related by 1.618. For very high-degree waves, sometimes the price multiples achieved by each of the three impulse waves are related to each other by powers of Fibonacci fractions, most commonly 5/3 and 8/5. Our analytical program, EWAVES, has used iconic counts to codify the distributions, and therefore the tendencies, of wave relationships in price and time.

PERSPECTIVE

Until a few years ago, the idea that market movements are patterned was controversial, but recent scientific discoveries have established that fractals permeate nature. This is the type of pattern identified in market movements by R.N. Elliott in 1938.

Most important to investors is that the Wave Principle often indicates in advance the relative *magnitude* of the next period of market progress or regress. Living in harmony with those trends can make the difference between success and failure in financial affairs.

To obtain a fuller understanding of the Wave Principle, read *Elliott Wave Principle* by A.J. Frost and Robert Prechter, available at elliottwave.com/books.

GLOSSARY

Alternation (guideline) – In an impulse wave, if wave two is a sharp correction, wave four will usually be a sideways correction, and vice versa.

Apex – Intersection of the two boundary lines of a contracting triangle or contracting diagonal.

Barrier Triangle – A triangle pattern where the B-D trendline is horizontal and the A-C trendline points in the direction of the main trend at next higher degree.

Channeling (guideline) – Impulse waves, zigzags and double zigzags often travel within a trend channel, whose boundaries are defined by parallel upper and lower price trendlines.

Combination – A sideways pattern composed of two corrective patterns linked by an intervening X wave.

Contracting Triangle – A triangle pattern whose A-C and B-D trendlines converge.

Corrective Wave – A three-wave pattern or combination of three-wave patterns.

Depth of Corrective Waves (guideline) – Within impulse waves, often the corrective waves – especially fourth waves – end in the price territory of the previous fourth wave of one lesser degree and usually at that fourth wave's termination point.

Diagonal – A motive wave that subdivides 3-3-3-3-3, progresses between converging lines, and whose wave 4 almost always ends in the price territory of wave 1. They occur in the first or fifth wave position.

Double Three – Combination that comprises two corrective wave patterns, labeled W and Y, linked by a corrective wave pattern labeled X.

Double Zigzag – Sharp wave pattern that comprises two zigzags, labeled W and Y, linked by a corrective wave pattern labeled X.

Equality (guideline) – When wave 3 of an impulse wave is extended, waves 1 and 5 will tend toward equality in terms of time and magnitude.

Expanded Flat – A version of a flat wave pattern where wave B goes beyond the start of wave A, and wave C goes beyond the end of wave A.

Expanding Triangle – A triangle wave pattern whose A-C and B-D trendlines diverge.

Extension – Elongated impulse wave whose subwaves, especially the actionary waves, are usually as long or longer than the waves at next higher degree.

Fibonacci relationships – These describe how the length of waves with respect to price and time are mathematically related to each other by the Fibonacci ratio of .618 or powers thereof.

Five – Used as a synonym for a motive wave.

Flat – Sideways corrective wave pattern, labeled A-B-C, that subdivides 3-3-5.

Guidelines – Characteristics of wave formation that usually – but don't always – occur.

Impulse wave – A motive wave pattern that subdivides 5-3-5-3-5. It usually travels within a parallel trend channel, and its wave 4 never ends in the price territory of wave 1.

Motive wave – A five-wave pattern that makes progress in the direction of the main trend, where wave 2 always retraces less than 100% of wave 1, and wave 3 can never be the shortest wave. The two kinds of motive wave are impulse and diagonal.

Orthodox top (or bottom) – Price level that represents the end of the wave pattern, not necessarily the most extreme price.

Regular Flat – A flat wave pattern where wave B terminates at about the start of wave A, and wave C ends just slightly past the end of wave A.

Right Look –When wave patterns conform to certain shapes, proportions and trendlines, they are said to have the "right look."

Rules – Characteristics of wave formation that always occur.

Running Flat – A flat wave pattern where wave B terminates well beyond the start of wave A, and wave C ends short of the end of wave A.

Running Triangle – A contracting triangle where wave B terminates beyond the start of wave A.

Sharp corrective wave – A zigzag or double zigzag, which forms a relatively steep angle and never registers a new price extreme beyond the previous wave that it is retracing.

Sideways corrective wave – A corrective wave pattern—a flat, triangle or double three—that is relatively horizontal in shape, and, before terminating, usually records a new price extreme beyond the previous wave that it is retracing.

Third-of-a-Third Impulse wave – The center of an impulse, normally the most powerful segment of an impulse wave.

Three – Used as a synonym for a corrective wave.

Throw-over – When wave 5 of an impulse wave terminates beyond the trendline of a parallel trend channel, or when wave 5 of a contracting diagonal terminates beyond the 1-3 trendline.

Triangle – A sideways corrective pattern, labeled A-B-C-D-E, that subdivides 3-3-3-3-3, where the initial subwaves are all zigzags or double zigzags.

Truncation – When wave 5 of a motive wave fails to exceed the end of wave 3, or when wave C of a zigzag fails to go beyond the end of wave A.

Zigzag – Sharp corrective wave pattern, labeled A-B-C, that subdivides 5-3-5.

Books